Coon Crazy

BIBBS

COON CRAZY

iUniverse books may be ordered through booksellers or by contacting:

iUniverse
1663 Liberty Drive
Bloomington, IN 47403
www.iuniverse.com
1-800-Authors (1-800-288-4677)

ISBN: 978-1-5320-4863-0 (sc)
ISBN: 978-1-5320-4866-1 (e)

Print information available on the last page.

iUniverse rev. date: 05/14/2018

Dedication

I dedicate this book to my good friend "Mule Man" who has passed away! He was a hunter and Outdoors man. He loved his wife, children, and grandchildren. He also loved his hunting dogs, horses, and mules.

Grandpa and Grandma

I was born in 1941 as a young country boy. I was always outdoors or in the woods. My father never hunted, but my mother's dad and a couple of her brothers hunted and trapped. My grandparents lived way back off any main roads on an old hill farm which had lots of acres. Most of it was timber woods. There were twenty or thirty acres of pasture and tillable ground. Grandpa always had hound dogs that ran loose. They would tree squirrels and ground hogs in the day time and possums and coons at night. Since he was home most of the time he would go shoot it out. Grandpa had a tobacco base which meant he could raise a certain amount of tobacco to sale. They also cut crossties, they would cut them down with a crosscut saw and then they would hew them out with a broad axe. They also cut and sold hickory billets to a factory in town. There they made axe and hammer handles with the wood. He always had a team of horses to do his work with. They always raised a big garden and a potato patch. He also raised hogs to butcher and a few to sell.

He would kill and scold them to remove the hair. They would quarter them up and salt it down in the smoke house.

They would take the trimmings and some of the other meat and grind it into sausage. They would always have fresh liver and onions on that day. Later Grandma would render the lard and make cracklings and sometime later they would make lye soap. They always had a milk cow and he would sell the calf for veal as this would bring good money. They seldom ate beef; Grandpa would find and cut a couple of bee trees for the honey. He also rented a few acres in the creek bottoms a few miles from where they lived. There he would raise corn for the animals. He would cut and shock the corn a little bit green. Then in the winter he would shuck it and feed the fodder to the cow and horses. They would grind some of it for cornmeal. He also raised a little bit of sorghum cane for sorghum molasses. Grandma would can lots of stuff from the garden. She also made black berry jelly and jam. She also had apple, peach, and persimmon trees.

They heated the old house with a sheet metal drum stove. Grandma would cook three meals everyday on a wood cook stove. They had to carry their drinking water from a spring about one eighth of a mile down over a hill. They only went to the store once a month for coffee, baking powder, salt and flour; just the necessities. They also had chickens and ducks. The chickens were mostly Bantams and big chicken cross. Some of the hens would hide their nest and lay twelve to fifteen eggs. Then she would set on them until they hatched. Then the hen would bring the chicks to the hen house. Grandma would catch the hen and tie a piece of string six or eight feet long on one leg. She would put an old wash tub or something for her to get under if it rained. This kept her from taking the chicks out in the weeds and something from getting them.

She kept them there until they had all their feathers and then she would turn the hen loose. They always had lots of eggs and fried chicken. Sometimes Grandma would kill an old hen that had stopped laying and make chicken and dumplings. They raised seven children, two girls and five boys. They never had electricity or running water and neither one of them ever learned to drive a car. My uncle's, mom's brothers, were always talking about coon hunting and how much fun it was. They caught possums and once in a while they would catch a coon. They were scarce back then. They had about all died off from distemper or some other disease. This was in the early nineteen forties.

My First Hunt

When I was about eight years old, we lived about seventy miles north of grandpa. We lived on a state highway and we had a few acres. Dad worked at a furniture factory and Mom stayed home. We had a milk cow, chickens, and raised a big garden.

One late summer's night we had some visitors that came to visit mom and dad. It was almost a full moon and I thought this would be a good night to go hunting since no one would miss me. I went outside and hollered for the dog and he came around the house and was ready to go! We called him Ole King. He was a big brown shepherd. He was a good watch dog and loved us kids. So we headed for the woods in back of the house. I walked down a big holler and went a long ways. Ole King stayed with me. He just looked around and I finally thought he doesn't know any more about coon hunting than I do.! So, we headed back home. As I got closer to the house I could hear mom and dad hollering for me. The visitors went home and they were looking for me. After dad got through with his belt on me it was a while before I would be going again.

My First Real Coon Hunt

At this time, we went to a one-room schoolhouse in the country. There were eight grades that went there; usually around thirty kids with three or four kids in each class. It had a big coal stove in the middle of the room and the teacher would take turns letting us kids bring coal from the shed behind the school. If it was winter time, we always had to have the buckets full before we went home in the evening. The teacher would come early in the morning and start the stove so it would be warm when we got there. The teacher would also send two of the bigger kids to the spring that was one eighth of a mile away to get the drinking water.

There were three boys and one girl in my class. One of the boys and I became good friends. His family had coon hounds and he invited me to come and spend the night with him and we would go hunting. A week or so later I went home with him. When the bus dropped us off at his house, the first thing I wanted to do was look at the dogs. They had two of the prettiest black and tan hounds I had ever seen. I helped my friend do his chores and later we had supper. I could hardly wait until dark. The boy's mom gave me some old clothes and a pair of gum boots since me and my friend wore the same size. His dad put on his clothes, lit the kerosene lantern, got the spotlight, and a twenty-two caliber single shot rifle.

He turned the dogs loose and we headed for a big cornfield up the bottoms a good ways from their house. After a while, one of the dogs started barking on a track. Then both dogs were barking and moving through the corn. Finally they reached the woods and shut up. Then all at once they both went to barking and it sounded different. My friend's dad said they are treeing which meant the coon went up a tree to get away from the dogs. We hurried and got there. One dog was standing with his front feet on the tree looking up and the other dog was sitting looking up and barking. My friend's dad took the spotlight and shined it up the tree and you could see the coon's eyes shining. So, he gave my friend the rifle and told him to shoot it out. At the crack of the gun, the coon fell out and the dogs grabbed him ready for a fight but he was already dead. We put the dogs on a leash and headed for the house because we had to go to school the next day.

I dreamed about coon hunting all night as I was hooked. I had to have some coon hounds.

Ole Ring

I had worked doing odd jobs for the neighbors. My younger brothers and I picked and sold raspberries and black berries - we got a dollar per gallon for black berries and two dollars a gallon for raspberries. I gave mom most of my money for school clothes and I kept back ten dollars for a twenty-two caliber rifle. I ordered it from a mail order catalog. It was a JC Higgins single shot that had to be manually cocked to fire. I bought a couple boxes of shells and I was ready for squirrel season.

Finally, the season came in and I was in the woods by daylight. I found a ridge that had lots of hickory trees and they were loaded with nuts. The gray squirrels had moved in and were really working on the nuts. I snuck up under one tree that had five or six squirrels in it. I shot at the closest one and missed. The rest of them left in a hurry---all you could see was tails flying everywhere. I shot at several more but missed them all. I was a crack shot with a BB gun so I thought the rifle was no good. That evening, I went back and took dad's twenty gauge shotgun and killed the limit which was five.

I spread the word around that I had a new rifle that I wanted to trade for a hunting dog.

A boy that I went to school with said he had a black cur dog that would chase any thing and he might trade for the rifle. I told him to bring the dog down sometime and we would take him hunting. He came down that weekend with the dog and we went hunting. There were lots of rabbits on our place. The dog was running and looking around and jumped a rabbit in a weed patch. Finally, the rabbit came out of the weeds and came down the fence row straight toward us. The boy shot at it with a four ten gauge shotgun. The rabbit didn't even slow down but ran up to where we were and fell over dead!

Later, when we dressed the rabbit we found only one pellet in its head. I asked the boy if he still wanted to trade and he said he did because they had too many dogs. So, I swapped the rifle for the dog, but I told the boy it did not shoot right. He said because it was new the sights needed adjusted. I thought a new gun would have been adjusted at the factory. We traded and I got a dog named Ring because he had a white ring around his neck. He was eighteen months old and was three-fourths cur and one-fourth bird dog.

On rainy or damp days, he would point and stay until you got to him and you could shoot a rabbit sitting. He would also tree squirrels. He would look and listen for them and then he would run up and sit down and watch them but I could never get him to bark. My younger brother who is two years younger than me started hunting and trapping with me that fall when hunting and trapping season came in. We set lots of traps. The DNR had brought in coons from the South and they mixed with the native coons around where we lived.

There was lots of spring bluffs and sinkholes. We set traps in groundhog holes for rabbits and Ole Ring would always go with us to the traps. He would run ahead and if he found something he would bark until we got there - he would not touch them.

He got really excited if we had a coon. We always carried a small cage with us made of wood and a wire lid on the top. We did this in case we caught rabbits. We would put them in the box and kill and dress them after school. One morning we caught a big coon; he was caught by his two front toes. We finally got him in the box and took him home. We had to hurry so we could catch the school bus. I took the trap off the coon and put him in the smokehouse. We never put much in there because it was full of junk and mom's fruit jars up on the shelves.

Ole Ring was running around like crazy, so I put him in the smokehouse and locked the door then we went to school. That evening when I got home I went to the smokehouse and everything was quiet. I opened the door and Ole Ring came out and the coon was dead. The shed was a total mess; fruit jars were everywhere with junk turned over and spilled. I went in and changed clothes and went back out and started cleaning up broken fruit jars. I swept and cleaned up everything. I took the broken jars and stuff down over the hill to a ditch where we put trash and covered it up.

Mom never did know about this, but during the summer when she started canning I did hear her say one time "I thought I had more jars than that".

I never did know what happened in that shed whether the dog killed the coon or a jar hit him on the head, but from that time on he was not afraid of them. If you sic him on one, he would run around till he could catch it by the back of the neck and then he would shake it until it was dead. He would catch possums, kill them and bring them back to you. We hunted a lot at night and I am sure he treed lots of game, but would not bark at the tree, therefore you could not find them.

Ole Blue

At the time I was fourteen years old my aunt and uncle live about ten miles from us. They came to visit one weekend and said a big Bluetick hound was staying at their house and they had tried to find out who owned him with no luck. The dog didn't have a collar on and they said if he was still there the next weekend, and I wanted him, they would bring him to me. I said that I wanted him so the following weekend they brought him over.

He was a big dog about eighteen months old he was a good looking hound. I had met an older man at the general store. I heard him and another guy talking about coon hunting and I asked them if they had any good dogs for sale. They said they were expensive and did not have anything for sale. He asked me if I had a dog and I told him I had just got a young Bluetick but did not know anything about him. He said when season comes in, which was just a few days away, he would take me hunting with him. I told him where we lived and he knew where it was. One night he came by with his son who was about thirty years old. He said if I wanted to go with them to get ready and get my dog. We went a long ways from home down in the river bottoms. We turned the dogs loose and walked for a while. It had been a rainy fall and water was everywhere. The dogs were all out hunting and all at once Ole Blue started to tree about one hundred feet from us. We shined the light over there and blue was standing in about a foot of water barking up the tree. We shined the spotlight up in the tree and saw two young coons. We waited for his dogs to come in and finally one did. After a while he said we might as well go on the coons are too small to shoot. I put Blue on a leash and led him a good piece before turning him loose. After a while, his dogs hit a track and finally treed. On the way there, we had to cross an old slew that was full of water. We walked up a way and found a big tree that had fallen across the water. My friend and I walked the log, but the old man had straddled it and was scooting across.

About halfway across he stopped to rest and all at once he reached in his bib overalls and got out his wallet and went to counting his money. He said I will give you one hundred dollars right now for that dog. That was the most money I had ever seen at one time, but I thought I had wanted a dog for so long I could not sell him. It turned out to be one of the biggest mistakes I've ever made.

We finished the hunt and went home. I was so proud of Blue. My younger brother and I hunted him about every night. Ole Blue never chased another coon. He went to running foxes!

As soon as he found a fox track he would run it all night. Sometimes he would run a gray fox and chase it down one ridge and back the other. My brother and I would hide and whip him if we caught him. But he got pretty smart and would shut up if he thought we were close.

I got a hunting supply catalog and ordered some Fox Stop. This stuff was to smell like a fox and the idea was to fasten the dog up with the scent on him in his box, with some air holes in it. He would eventually hate the smell. My aunt and uncle that lived about fifty miles away were planning to come and stay with us over the weekend and he would bring his dog and go hunting. He had a medium eared black and tan that was a good coon dog. They came up on Saturday so we planned on going that night. I knew a good place to go about five miles from where we lived - big woods with corn all around. I got Ole Blue out of his box and loaded him in the truck.

When we got to where we were going, I caught blue and put some more Fox Stop on his collar pad. When he hit the ground he started barking and went plumb out of hearing range. My uncle rolled on the ground laughing and said "he will never catch that fox!"

I guess with that Fox Stop he thought he was after one. We treed three coons with his dog. Later, when we got ready to go home, we hadn't seen or heard from Blue. I told my uncle let's go home and I never saw him again.

The Dog Traders

My dad worked with a guy at the furniture factory who liked to coon hunt. He had a pair of Red Bones and he raised and sold the pups as well as traded them. He said he would come to our place to go hunting some night.

So one Friday night, he came down and we went hunting. They sure were pretty dogs. The dogs hit a couple of tracks that ended in the ground, but we did not tree any coons. I asked him if he had any pups or a good dog for sale, but he said he didn't at the time. He said he was going to a dog trader on Sunday evening and that I could go with him and maybe fine something.

So Sunday we went to the dog trader's – he lived on the edge of a very small town. He must have had thirty or forty dogs. There were dogs tied up everywhere and a lot of them were running loose. I thought he must be the dog catcher of that small town. He had a big black kettle about thirty gallons or so and he put garbage from restaurants and stores in it. He would cook this and add corn meal and this is how the dogs were fed.

There were several hunters there. Some were looking for rabbit dogs, some were looking for squirrel dogs, and some were looking for coon dogs. When you would ask if a dog was good or not, he would reply "the guy I got it from said it was a good dog".

I spotted a medium sized Bluetick female that looked like she might do something. I paid the guy thirty-five dollars for her and headed home. This guy said he would be going back in two weeks and if she didn't suit me I could trade her for another dog. My brother and I hunted her and Ring most of the two weeks. One night, Ring caught a possum on the ground. We put it up a bush and hissed and petted her and tried to get her interested. After a while, we shot the rifle and that was the last we saw of her until we got home. She was gun shy.

Two weeks later, the guy stopped by and we went back to the Dog Trader. I found another dog that I liked the look of and asked how he wanted to trade. He wanted my dog and ten dollars. He asked me about my dog and I said "the guy I got it from said it was a good one."

I paid him the difference and went home.

This dog was as bad as the first dog. Two weeks later we went back and I found a big black and tan. He was fat and slick. This time the trader wanted another ten dollars. I traded with him and went home.

We started hunting him and Ring. He would walk along with us then he would decide to see what Ring was doing.

He would find his track and bark all the way to him. Then he would come back to us and by this time we had moved on, so he would find our track and bark all the way to us. This went on the whole time you were hunting. We took him several nights and it was the same. A few nights went by and we decided to go again. This time we tied him up in the barn and just took Ring. He started barking as soon as we left. We had got about a half-mile from home and I told my brother he is getting closer.

Dad and mom had gone to bed and could not go to sleep for the barking. That was the reason I tied him in the barn away from the house. Dad got out of bed and went out and turned him loose. I told my brother to get ready with that light. When he gets close enough I am going to shoot him. But when he got there he was wagging his tail and had a look on his face like why did you leave me at home. I did not have the heart to shoot him. A few days later, I called my friend that took me to the dog trader and I gave the dog to him. He said he would trade him for something. I had decided I did not want any more dogs from that dog trader.

Ole Jack

One Sunday my dad and mom took my dad's mom down to see her brother. He lived about twenty-five miles away in the river bottom. In the summer we would take grandma down quite often. He was a retired farmer and hunter. He had a son that liked to coon hunt. Before going to the army, he had to get rid of his dogs. All except Jack who actually belonged to his dad. After his son came home from the army he drank a lot; he lost a leg in the army. He still lived with his dad and mom as he never married. When they were down there visiting, dad's uncle asked my dad if my brother and I were still hunting. Dad told him we were, but didn't have too much of a dog. He told dad that he would like for us to have Jack. He said that if we came down on a Wednesday night about seven p.m., his son would be at the tavern drinking, and that would be a good time to come get the dog. He said that last week his boy had been to the tavern and got drunk. He came home and went hunting. Later a neighbor came to their house and said that their boy was passed out in the ditch along the county road. They were afraid that he was going to freeze to death. He said that if he got rid of the dog the boy would stop hunting. So, the following Wednesday night we got down there at seven p.m.

Sure enough the boy was at the tavern. He said take this dog and give him a good home. He said he is the best coon dog in the country. He said when you cross the river going home to throw the collar in the river. He said that if the boy ever found out where the dog went he would take all the blame. The dog actually belonged to him, not his boy. We thanked him for the dog and went home. He was a medium-eared black and tan with a frosty muzzle. He was four years old. My brother and I thought we had finally gotten a coon dog.

We kept the dog tied and didn't hunt him for a couple of days so he would get use to us. Then we started hunting him. He would stay with us but wouldn't do anything. We must have hunted him thirty days or so. Still nothing. I told my brother that we had been through all this trouble and the dog was worthless.

I had a Redtick pup that was about six months old. I told my brother lets go hunting and take this pup. So we went to this good place. Corn on one side of the gravel road, big woods on the other. We walked about two miles down this access road to a state forest. We were on our way back when a possum crossed the road in front of us. My brother ran him down. We took him up in the woods off the road and put him up a bush and tried to get the Redtick pup to fool with it. We petted and hissed, but he was not that much interested. Jack was there looking on. So we left the possum up the bush and headed home. We got about one hundred yards away and Jack started barking. We went back and he was barking at the treed possum. I told my brother we might as well shake it out to him. He's no good anyway. So we shook it out, and let him get it. Then we took the possum and headed home. Jack crossed the road into the cornfield and started barking. He ran through the corn field and crossed the road and went up the hill and sat down barking treed. We went up there and shined the light, and he had a big coon. We shot it out and went back to the road. Ole Jack went back in the corn and opened up again. This time on the other side of the corn. There was a big creek with a few big trees. He had treed again another big coon. We shot it out, put a leash on him, and went home. From that night on we had a coon dog.

We caught lots of coons with him. He never ran any kind of off game. If there were no coons running, after a while he would tree a possum and you had to shoot it or shake it out. He would just shake and lay it down. You could not call him off the tree or lead him for a while or he would wait till you got a long way off then go back. This aggravated me some, but when he treed he would stay all night, you did not have to run to the tree. We found out later that the guy had whipped him for treeing possums. It almost ruined him. As he got older he quit treeing possums all together.

The Lost Dog

By this time I was old enough to get my driver's license. I quit school and went to work for a contractor building houses. I bought an old Chevy car and took the backseat out of it. Then I closed it off from the front seat to the back. With the room in the back floorboard and trunk I had plenty of room for carpentry tools and dogs. This was our hunting buggy! One night I took Jack and a pup up to a state forest. The forest had lots of big timber. I had hunted there before and caught some big blackish coons. They were long legged and could really run. I got there a little after dark and turned the dogs loose. With Jack you did not have to walk. I would go out in the woods about fifty feet, light the lantern and go back to the car. After about ten minutes Jack opened on track and ran a good ways and treed. He had two coons up one tree. I shot them out, and about that time it started snowing. I put a leash on him and started to the car. The snow was really coming down and it was getting slick. Carrying two big coons, rifle, and a lantern, I turned Jack loose. I tried to make him stay with me. After a while he snuck off. He knew coons were really moving around. I finally got to the car and he wasn't with me.

I put the pup, coons, and lantern in the car. I waited about twenty minutes. I never heard a sound. There were lots of big hills and hollers, and Jack must have treed out of hearing distance. The snow was getting heavier and the road slicker. I didn't know if I could make it home or not. I took my hunting coat off and put it about fifty feet up in the woods for him to lie on and he would know that I would be back for him.

Finally I got home. It had snowed five or six inches. The next morning I went to work. We were setting trusses on a building and I had to be there. After work I went back to where I had been hunting the night before. I called and called and walked up to where I had left my coat. There were no tracks around it. I picked up my coat and stayed around there until dark, then went home. I went back every evening the rest of that week.

The weekend finally came and Saturday morning I was there at daylight. I checked every fence that was along the boundary of the state forest, shot the rifle, and still no dog. I went back a few more times, I finally gave up.

There had been a few old homesteads in there before the state had bought those years ago. I just figured he may have fell in an old well somewhere, or somebody had stolen him. I lost him on a Wednesday night. The next Wednesday night, seven days later, the weather had warmed up. The snow was gone. So my brother and I decided to go hunting. I loaded his pup and Ole Ring, we headed back to the state forest where I had lost Jack. I knew there was still coons there. We got there and parked in the same pull off. Before I could get the car shut off something was scratching on the car door. It was Jack. He was as glad to see us as we were to see him. We petted and made over him, by this time we didn't want to go hunting. We went home. Mom and dad couldn't figure out why we were home so early. Before we could tell them anything, mom said I have found Jack! A guy about ten miles away from where you lost him has got him. I said no he doesn't, we have him. I always kept a collar with a name plate on him. I didn't have a telephone number on the plate just our address. The guy I got him from said the only way you could chain him was to put a chain choker behind the leather collar. He was so broad in his shoulders and neck he would slip a leather collar off.

The next evening, I called that guy that found him and said I hear you have my dog. He said he did have him, but all he had now was the collar. I told him the dog had come back where I left him. He could not believe the dog could do that. He lived on the other side of a small town from where the dog was. The dog had to cross two state highways and all kinds of roads.

He was out driving his new Jeep in the forest snow about ten o'clock the next morning when he saw Jack. He said the dog was standing in the middle of the road and looked lost. He picked him up and took him home and tied him up. He said that Jack stayed that day and left the next night. He had written the letter the day that he picked Jack up and put the letter in the box. It wasn't picked up until the next day. I don't know why it took so long to reach us but it did. I thanked him for picking up the dog and letting us know. I told him to throw the collar away. I was sure glad he was an honest guy.

The Night of the UFOs

One night late in the hunting season. It had been almost a full moon. The moon would be going down at three-thirty a.m. I got up at three a.m. I got ready and loaded Ole Jack and took off. I went down the road a couple of miles from home to a place called Hudson Spring Bluff. There was big timber and a lot of big old hollow beach trees. It was a cold frost night. I parked and let Jack out. I took the lantern and walked a little ways from the car and set down on a stump. As a coon hunter you see lots of things in the sky at night. I have seen falling stars and meteorites that go all the way across the sky. I have seen the northern lights and have even seen fox-fire. That is where a log or piece of wood is going through a decaying stage and giving off a florescent glow.

I was sitting on the stump and the moon was going down. I had not lit the lantern yet and I was looking up at the sky. I could see ten or eleven white lights in a row. This was about the time everybody was talking about and seeing UFOs. Sometimes they would go out for a while. Then they would come back on all in a row. They didn't make any noise and were not moving. It finally got completely dark and I kept watching them. I was sure they were UFO's. After about thirty minutes Jack came back satisfied coons weren't running. I put a leash on Jack and just sat there. After it got real dark I could tell when the lights came on. The woods lit up from the light. I did not believe in UFOs but I could not figure this out.

After a while I loaded my rifle. I had retired the old single shot twenty-two and bought a new Remington Nylon sixty-six. It shot fifteen shells loaded in the stock. I put Jack and the lantern in the car. There was a big hill I had to climb; I was going to the top of the hill so I could see better.

The closer I got to the top of the hill the brighter they were when they came on. When I finally got to the top it was pitch dark. I just stood there and waited. Finally a light breeze from the east started blowing. The lights would come on and I was real close to them. I walked a little farther and saw a big power line. It was one that went from one substation to another. As the wind would blow it got some small tree branches close enough to cause static electricity to light them up. But it made no noise. I knew then why Jack had not found any coon tracks. They do not like to run when the wind is from the east. If I had not walked up that hill I would have sworn I saw UFOs.

The Ghost Coon

There was a place not far from home where everyone hunted. There was a creek that was good size but there were riffles where you could wade across. On the other side there was a cornfield and big woods.

At the first of the season people would catch all the young and easy coons. But there was one coon that no one could catch. They called him the ghost coon. When you went hunting there the dogs would usually hit his track and after a while it would blow up.

I had never hunted there after I got Jack. So, my brother and I decided to go there and see what Jack could do. The old coon would come out of his den and lay a big circle. Then he would feed inside the circle. When a dog would hit his track and open, he would head for the creek and home.

Ole Jack had grown up and was raised in the river bottoms. He was use to the water. When we got there it didn't take long until Jack opened on track. He ran him out of the corn to the creek. Jack would not open on track till he was moving. After getting to the creek we did not hear from him for a while. Then he started barking treed but he sounded funny. We walked up to where he was barking and there was a big pool of water. About twenty feet across and five feet or six feet deep with a big sycamore tree on the creek bank. The top had blown out years earlier and there was one big limb that hung down close to the water in the middle of the big pool. Jack was swimming around that limb barking. That was where the coon went up. Jack finally came up to us on the bank and we put a leash on him. I walked to the car and got a rope and went back. I threw it over a big limb on the bank side of the tree. I climbed up to where I could look down in the tree. The coon was all the way down to the ground. I blew on the coon squaller and he looked at me. He was the biggest coon I ever saw. We talked about going home and getting an axe to chop a hole in the tree, but we decided that we could not kill a coon like that. All the hunters around said that nobody could tree the ghost coon. We never said anything but we knew we could tree him anytime we wanted. I think he eventually died of old age.

The Big Cat

One night I took Ole Jack and a young dog to a place I had never been. From the road it was about three or four miles any direction to any roads or houses. It had lots of big timber and rock bluffs. The weather had been bad with lots of snow. It had warmed up and melted most of the snow. There were little patches of snow here and there. I walked a good ways from the truck and Jack opened up. He had hit a track and ran almost out of hearing and treed. I started to him. I heard the young dog bark a few times. As I got about two hundred feet from the tree, it jumped out and the race was on again. I have heard of coons doing this but I have never had it happen to me. The dogs ran a long ways and treed again. As I got close to the tree, it jumped out of the tree and the race was on again. This time I took off after the dogs and after a long race, Jack quit barking. The young dog was barking kind of funny. As I got to the young dog, he was barking around this big hole in the bluff. It had a big rock ledge over it and there was still some snow that had blown in there. Ole Jack would not bark at something in the ground. I looked at the snow and found some cat tracks that were as big as the dog's tracks. Now I knew whatever it was, it was not a coon. I had heard of some sightings of a mountain lion or some kind of a big cat in this area. I put a leash on the dogs and headed for the truck. I never did go back in that area again.

The Honey Tree

One Fall my brother and I went coon hunting. The season had just come in. it had been an extremely dry and hot summer. It was warm enough that we did not have to wear a jacket. We went to the creek bottoms and was walking around the edge of a big corn field. There was a fence row with a few small trees and it was light enough that you could see without a walking light. As we were standing and waiting for the dogs to find a track, I could bulk an object in a wild cherry tree. We walked over and shined the light up in the tree. The object was only about twelve feet off the ground. It was a brown ball and as we were looking at it, you could see it moving. We threw a dirt clod and hit it; there were bees going everywhere and you could see the honey comb. There had been a swarm of honey bees land on this small limb and stayed there making honey. I told my brother let's get out of here and the first real frosty night we will come back and get the honey. About a week or so later, the temperature dropped down and we had a heavy frost. We went back over there that night and took a small tarp, plastic bags, and a pole saw that would reach twelve feet. When we got there the bees were still there and we put the tarp under where they would fall. Then we sawed the limb off. When it hit the ground most of the bees fell off and we shook the rest of them off as they were dying anyways. There were seven or eight pounds of the whitest pure honey you ever saw. We bagged it up and headed for home. We thanked the Lord for the honey but felt sorry for the bees.

The Longest Race

The guy I was working for bought five or six lots on a five-acre private lake. We built a cabin for him as a get a way on weekends. He was also going to build cabins on the other lots and sell them. The lake was six years old. It had been stocked with channel catfish, bass, and hybrid blue gill. My boss had a small pontoon boat, up there all the time, at his dock. You had to be a landowner or live there to have the right to use the lake. Since another guy and I worked there, we could fish there anytime we wanted. We caught lots of fish there. There was a general store a quarter mile down the road on a state highway and we would go there for lunch sometimes. Across the road from the store was state property. It had a big cornfield that a farmer had rented from the state. Beyond it was a small creek and big woods. I walked over to the creek one day on lunch break and I saw coon tracks everywhere. I knew that when coon season came in, I would be there.

Season finally came that fall. One Saturday night my brother and I went up there. It was about twenty miles from where we lived. I wanted to be there at midnight so there would be less traffic on the highway where we were hunting. We just took one dog, Ole Jack. We parked at the store and crossed into the cornfield. We went about fifty feet out into the corn, stopped and turned Ole Jack loose. I looked at my watch and it was exactly midnight. About that time, Jack opened on a track. He ran up and down and all around in that corn. I told my brother he must be running a rabbit. Every so often he would come close to us. I told my brother to blow out the lantern and spread out and maybe we could see what he was running.

After a while, I heard something coming and it was breathing heavy. I turned the flashlight on and it was a big coon. As soon as the light hit him, he jumped over several cornrows and went the other way. We decided to try and shoot him. We moved over to where it sounded like the dog was coming towards us. As he got close enough, my brother flipped on the light and I shot at him and missed. It kind of messed Ole Jack up some--us shooting. After a few minutes the race was on again. We thought we'd better quit shooting or we might hit the dog. There were so many tracks going everywhere; zig zagging and crossing each other. Jack would shut up until he got it figured out. There was a narrow patch of trees close to the creek. I told my brother if he ever comes out of the corn, that is where it will be. After several more laps through the corn the coon came out right in front of us and Jack was right behind him. The coon jumped in the creek, it was just a little pool of water five or six inches deep. He was ready for a fight. Jack was running around that pool baying him. I caught Jack and shot the coon. Jack was too tired to fight. I looked at my watch and it was one fifty-five a.m. Jack had run that coon one hour and fifty-five minutes. I will never know why the coon wouldn't come out of the corn. I think in all the excitement he got lost.

Ole Blaze

I had built a new house for a guy that worked at a Factory. He had been there for many years. I told him I was getting tired of the building trade. You had to work in the hot sun in the summer and cold in the winter. Health insurance was getting higher and it was harder to get good help. The factory had started hiring more people. The guy put in a good word for me and I got hired on. I liked it right off. They had good insurance and all kinds of benefits. I became friends with a guy that coon hunted. He had a coon and squirrel dog which was registered as a mountain cur but it was mostly a black and tan hound. Ole Blaze had a little bit of white between his eyes and that is the reason he called him Blaze. He was a good coon dog but the best squirrel dog I ever saw. This guy's name was Mule Man because he had a hunting mule. We hunted together quite a bit. We were older and could not climb the hills like we once did. So, I bought a coon hunting mule. That was the way to hunt. We would usually go to the state ground or some place that didn't have any fences. You could take your coffee, sandwiches, rifle, and whatever and go all night.

One day in squirrel season, we loaded the mules and Blaze in the stock trailer and went to a national forest. We got there and unloaded and started hunting at nine a.m. Ole Blaze treed twenty-one times that day. We must have seen fifteen of these squirrels. Some went into den trees and some of them went from tree to tree and left.

One time Blaze treed on a big beech tree. The squirrel jumped from tree to tree and came down to the ground fifty yards away and ran off. Ole Blaze just watched him run off and went back to barking up the tree that the squirrel had climbed. He would not pull from the tree until you called him off. Mule Man won several hunts with him for the "best combination dog"---Coons at night and squirrels by day. Ole Blaze died when he was ten years old. He was the kind of tree dog everyone wanted.

Ole Kate the Coon Hunting Mule

My friend had this mule. She was about fifteen years old when he got her. She was the best mule I ever saw. She was fifty-four inches tall, medium built and a grey color. She had been broke and trained by an old man that had raised her. She was not a kid's mule. Though she was gentle enough, she had too much go for a small kid. Kate would walk, trot or cantor as good as any horse I ever saw. She would neck-reign almost like she had power steering. You could lead dogs with her, shoot a shotgun off her and she wouldn't even flinch. She had been squirrel and coon hunted with all her life. When the dogs treed, all you had to do was say "let's go" and without guidance she would go to them. When you were done hunting all you had to do was turn her a couple circles, turn her loose, and tell her to "Go home" and she would take you home or to the truck.

There were times we would hunt all night and then go home and one of our friends would call and want to go trail riding. I had a good mule, but after riding her all night she seemed tired. I would usually take a horse, but my friend always rode Kate. After trail riding all day, she still had lots of go left in her.

One day we were trail riding in a state park. When lunchtime came, we stopped at a rest area in the park which had a hitching rail and picnic tables. There were eight riders already there eating. They all rode big fancy horses and could not believe my friend was riding that little mule. Mule Man told them that his little mule would still be going when their horses were all worn out. My friend was proud of Kate and he liked to brag on her. He told them several stories about how good she was. You could tell they thought he was just bragging. They were still there when we got ready to go. There was a gravel area with a swale through the middle. Ole Kate was standing with her front feet on one side and her back feet on the other. As my friend started to get on, his feet rolled on the gravel and he fell directly under the mule and made a big noise as he was trying to catch himself. It scared the other horses and a couple of them broke loose. Ole Kate never moved a muscle as he wallowed around trying to get up. Once he got up and got on, the other riders all tried to buy Kate. One of the older men said, "Boy, that is a good mule".

My friend kept her till she was thirty years old. He did not want to see her die. He, more or less, gave her to a young girl that just starting riding. My friend let her ride Kate and they hit right off. She promised to take good care of her till she died. About five years later she called my friend and said Kate had died. She then thanked him again and told him how much she loved Ole Kate.

Mule Man

Mule man and I became good friends. We hunted, fished, camped, trail rode many miles, mushroom hunted, cut wood, and helped each other in many ways. I knew him over twenty-five years, ate many meals at his house. His wife was a good cook. We watched each other's children grow up. In all those years we never had a cross word between us. Mule man passed away and I miss him and think about him often. He had several names: mule man, bull, mule skinner and mushroom hound. I called him friend. "Best Friend".

Ole Red

When my oldest son was in his thirties, he got a redbone pup. He had always loved redbones since he saw the movie *Where the Red Fern Grows*. It was a pretty dark male pup. He had it in the woods when it was six months old. He would take him mushroom hunting, fishing, and digging ginseng. We started coon hunting him when he was a year old and he got to trying to run a track. When he was two years old he got to running fairly good. The other dogs would run off and leave him, but he would not quit his own track. He got to treeing some. The third year, he was running and treeing all by himself. He had a soft voice that would not scare a coon. He could tree a coon the easiest I ever saw. It seemed he never got excited. He was good on lay up coons. I've had dogs that would scream and squall and were fast but would scare every coon in the country to death. They would go in a den tree or ground. My boy patch-hunted him a lot. You could let him out, he would check out a cornfield or patch of woods and come back ready to go somewhere else. He caught lots of coons with him. When he was seven years old, the boy let him out at a cornfield. He had hunted there many times before. It was on a county road that had very little traffic on it. Red hit a coon in the corn and it ran across the road. He got hit and killed by one of the few cars that went down that road. My boy still misses that dog.

Little Jack

I had a little dog. She was one-half beagle and one-half fox terrier. I had got her for the kids to play with from a friend of mine. She was not interested in hunting. I had another friend that had a good squirrel dog. He was one-half fox terrier and one-half Australian shepherd. I bred the female we had to him and she had five pups. We kept two and gave the rest away. One pup was black and tan with a little white on him. We called him Jack. The other pup was spotted. We called him Drum. They ran loose all the time. We lived in the country where everyone let their dogs run loose. Drum was a visitor. He liked to roam all over the County. One day they tore into the neighbor's rabbit pin and killed his rabbit. He came out and as they were running off, he shot and killed Drum. He came and told me about it. He was sorry about shooting the dog, but he could not have them killing his animals. I told him I would have done the same thing. I paid him for the rabbit and tied Jack for a few days. After I let him loose, he never did go to the neighbors anymore. I tried to make a squirrel dog with him, but he was not interested so he was just a pet.

My boy had Ole Red back then. Sometimes he would come

to my house and want me to take him some place and drop him off. He would hunt through the woods to my house. If he was within hearing distance of my house and Jack heard Red barking, he would go to them as fast as he could. He would usually be there before the coon was shot out. He only weighed about twenty five pounds, but he would fight a coon as big as he was. He really hated them. After a while, my boy started taking him with them. Ole Red rode in the dog box, but Little Jack got to ride up front in the truck. Lots of times he would tree before Red did. After Red got killed, Jack was his only dog.

He was a smart little dog. He got to where he would not let me catch him if he thought I was going to tie him up. Anyone else could catch him but me. Lots of times, if I was sitting on the porch or in the yard he would come up to me, set down, and take his paw and touch me so I would pet him. He knew the sound of my boy's truck. I think he could hear it a mile away. By the time my boy would get to the house, Little Jack would be waiting in the driveway ready to go hunting. He was still mouthed and would not bark till he had treed. They caught coons in the bluffs and places where an open-mouthed dog could not. I kept him until he was ten years old. He developed a tumor in his throat and he coughed all the time. The vet said it would be best to put him down. The vet gave him a shot and instantly it was over. It was one of the hardest things I have ever had to do. I took him home and my boy came up and buried him somewhere in the woods.

Ole Katy

I bought this medium sized Bluetick female. She was mixed with some kind of cur dog. I got her at a water race and treeing contest. She was about eighteen months old. She won all her heats in the water races and treeing contests that she was in. She had never been coon hunted in the wild, but she hated a coon.

I had built a new house and moved to a new location. There was a big corn field a quarter of a mile up a railroad track. It was in the late summer and dog running season was still in. After dark I would lead her up to the corn field and turn her lose. There were lots of coons there. She would go out into the corn and eventually you would hear a coon squall and her barking. She would catch them on the ground. but If it was a very big coon she could not kill it. The coon would run and go up the nearest tree and she would tree it. My oldest son was ten years old and he would go with me most of the time. He would climb the tree if it was not too big and shake it out. I would let her watch it run off. After a few minutes I would turn her loose and she would run and tree it again. We did this several times before hunting season came in. When fall and hunting season came in, we had a coon dog. She would only bark if it was a hot track. She was smart. If you hunted her in a place where the coons would go in the ground, after a few different times of running that same coon, she would not bark till the coon was treed. Lots of times in the latter part of hunting season when coons were rutting, I would get up early in the morning and turn her loose. Then I would go back into the house to make coffee and eat breakfast. Then I would get ready and go outside and she would be treed somewhere. I would go shoot it out and by the time I got back home it would be daylight. I hunted her several years and caught lots of coons with her. I finally sold her to a friend of mine and he kept her till she died.

I coon hunted over fifty plus years. I have had lots of good dogs. Some I bought. Some I raised. But none of them have given me the pleasure I had with Ring and Ole Jack. Ring got to barking, treed in his old age. If you hunted him by himself, he would just bark enough to get you to the tree. I kept both dogs till they died. I am seventy-seven years old and physically unable to hunt anymore. My oldest boy started hunting with me when he was six years old. Now he has a family and dogs of his own and I guess you could say he's Coon Crazy.

That is what people said about my younger brother and I.

The End.

My hunting Mule.

Future hunting mule. One day old.

Printed in the United States
By Bookmasters